AF868741

LEVEL E

Soaring Scores

NYS Social Studies with DBQs

Reviewers

Doreen A. Andersen, M.S.
Smithtown School District
Nesconset Elementary School
Nesconset, New York

Katherine E. Neirotti, M.A.
Historian
Torah Academy
of Suffolk County (TASC)
Commack, New York

Gail Wolczanski, M.S.
5th-Grade Teacher/Consultant
Oxford Road Elementary School
New Hartford, New York

STECK-VAUGHN BERRENT
A Harcourt Company

www.steck-vaughn.com

Acknowledgments

Editorial Manager:	Karen Bischoff
Supervising Editor:	Carol Traynor
Editor:	Caren Churchbuilder
Editorial Team:	Edward Nasello Christy Yaros
Editorial Development:	McCormick Associates, Inc.
Art Director:	Frank Bruno
Design and Production:	Susan Geer Associates, Inc.
Design Associate:	Gregory Silverman
Illustrator:	Jane Kendall
Cover Design:	
Art Direction	Frank Bruno
Design	Jean-Paul Vest Bradford Foltz

Photo credits

Cover: (immigrants on Ellis Island) ©Bettmann/CORBIS, (map of China) ©Image Bank, (Statue of Liberty) ©Bettmann/CORBIS; p. 21 ©Stone; p. 27 ©The Granger Collection; p. 37 Courtesy the Library of Congress; p. 53 ©The New-York Historical Society; p. 55 ©National Park Service; p. 57 ©Brown Brothers.

Additional photography by: Corbis, Eyewire, Photodisc

Soaring Scores NYS Social Studies with DBQs: Level E

STECK-VAUGHN BERRENT
A Harcourt Company

www.steck-vaughn.com

ISBN 0-7398-3995-0

Published by Steck-Vaughn/Berrent Publications, a division of Steck-Vaughn Company.

3 4 5 6 7 8 9 RP 05 04 03 02

TABLE OF CONTENTS

NEW YORK STATE SOCIAL STUDIES STANDARDS

STANDARD 1 History of the United States and New York

Use a variety of intellectual skills to demonstrate your understanding of major ideas, eras, themes, developments, and turning points in the history of the United States and New York.

STANDARD 2 World History

Use a variety of intellectual skills to demonstrate your understanding of major ideas, eras, themes, developments, and turning points in world history and examine the broad sweep of history from a variety of perspectives.

STANDARD 3 Geography

Use a variety of intellectual skills to demonstrate your understanding of the geography of the interdependent world in which we live—local, national, and global—including the distribution of people, places, and environments over the Earth's surface.

STANDARD 4 Economics

Use a variety of intellectual skills to demonstrate your understanding of how the United States and other societies develop economic systems and associated institutions to allocate scarce resources, how major decision-making units function in the United States and other national economies, and how an economy solves the scarcity problem through market and nonmarket mechanisms.

STANDARD 5 Civics, Citizenship, and Government

Use a variety of intellectual skills to demonstrate your understanding of the necessity for establishing governments; the governmental system of the United States and other nations; the United States Constitution; the basic civic values of American constitutional democracy; and the roles, rights, and responsibilities of citizenship, including avenues of participation.

KINDS OF QUESTIONS

The New York State Social Studies Test includes three different types of questions. *Soaring Scores NYS Social Studies with DBQs* will help prepare you to answer these questions.

Multiple-Choice Questions

You will have multiple-choice questions in the beginning of the test. You must select the correct answer to a question from four choices. There is only one correct answer. Find the correct answer and then fill in the circle for that answer. The circle will either be at the bottom of the page or, in the Test section, it will be on a separate Answer Sheet.

Constructed-Response Questions

You will have constructed-response questions in the middle of the test. For these questions, you will not have choices to pick from. You must figure out the answer on your own and write it down in the space after the question.

You will answer a group of questions based on some information that is given to you. This information may be a map, chart, picture, or paragraph. Here is how you should answer these questions:

FIRST – Look at the information given to you at the top of the page. Try to figure out what the information is and what it tells you.

NEXT – Read the first question under the information. This question will be about the information you just looked at.

NEXT – Look at the information at the top of the page again and try to figure out the answer to the question. The information will ALWAYS help you find the answer to these questions.

LAST – Write your answer in the space after the question. Make sure you answer the question as completely as possible. Use supporting details. For some of these questions you may get partial credit. So, even if your answer is not totally correct, you may get some points.

Continue to read the remaining questions on the page. Use the information at the top of the page to help you find the answer. Then fill in the space after each question as completely as possible.

Document-Based Questions

You will have one document-based question at the end of the New York State Social Studies Test. There are two parts to a document-based question, Part A and Part B. The steps to answering Part A are just like those for constructed-response questions. You must answer some questions after each document, based on the information in the document. Here is a review from page 5 on how to answer the questions in **Part A**:

FIRST – Study the document given to you at the top of the first page.

NEXT – Read the first question under the document.

NEXT – Look at the document at the top of the page again. Try to figure out the answer to the question based on the information.

LAST – Write your answer as completely as possible in the space after the question. Use supporting details. Remember, you may get partial credit. Even if your answer is not totally correct, you may get some points.

Continue to answer the remaining questions for the document, if there are any. Always remember to look at the document to help you figure out the answer.

Once you have answered all of the questions for the first document, turn to the next page and do the same for the next document. Follow the same steps in answering the questions. Keep doing this until you have answered ALL of the questions for ALL of the documents that you are given.

Part B of the document-based question is an essay question. You must now use the answers you wrote for each of the documents to write an essay on a particular topic.

REMEMBER!

It is very important to use your answers from Part A to write the essay in Part B. You may use some things you already knew, but the purpose of a document-based essay question is to use what you found in the documents that you were given. Try to use as many documents as you can in your essay.

The essay is scored on a rubric like the one on the next page. Look at this rubric so that you can see what kind of an answer will give you the top score. Talk to your teacher about the rubric and ask any questions that you have about document-based questions.

DBQ GENERIC RUBRIC

written by the New York State Education Department*

4

- Answers all aspects of the task by using the documents and may bring in relevant outside information related to the documents
- Consistently uses accurate data
- Develops ideas fully, using such supporting evidence as examples, reasons, details, explanations, and generalizations that are relevant and appropriate
- Demonstrates a logical plan of organization and coherence in the development of ideas
- Consistently expresses ideas clearly

3

- Answers most aspects of the task by using the documents
- Generally uses accurate data
- Develops ideas satisfactorily with adequate supporting evidence
- Develops an answer, using a general plan of organization
- Generally expresses ideas clearly

2

- Answers some aspects of the tasks by using some of the documents
- Uses some accurate data
- Demonstrates weakness in development of ideas with little supporting evidence
- Attempts to organize an answer but is weak and goes off the topic
- Attempts to express ideas clearly

1

- Does not use information to support ideas or uses information which is not relevant
- Shows limited understanding of the task
- Fails to use documents or only vaguely refers to the documents
- Lacks a plan of organization
- Does not express ideas clearly

0

- Uses no accurate data
- Fails to answer question or response is totally unrelated to topic
- Illegible or so many words cannot be read that no sense can be made of the response
- Blank paper
- Is incoherent; i.e., words are legible but syntax is so garbled that no sense can be made of the response

* Grateful acknowledgment is made to the New York State Education Department for permission to reprint its document-based generic rubric.

MODELED INSTRUCTION

STANDARD 1 History of the United States and New York

Directions: In this section you will answer questions based on the history of the United States and New York. Questions 1 through 5 are followed by four choices. Read each question carefully. Decide which choice is the correct answer. Mark your answer at the bottom of the page by filling in the circle that has the same letter as the answer you have chosen.

1 Which had a powerful effect on the way of life of the Plains Indians?

A the horse

B coastal waters full of salmon

C frozen land and water

D large forests

HINT Look for a key word like "Plains." Think of what you know about the American Plains. They are in the Midwest, far from either coast, and have few trees.

2 Which name below might be the name of an Iroquois clan, or group of related people?

A New Yorker

B Algonquin

C Wolf

D Wampum

HINT Remember that each Iroquois clan took the name of an animal.

Answers

1 Ⓐ Ⓑ Ⓒ Ⓓ

2 Ⓐ Ⓑ Ⓒ Ⓓ

Go On

Base your answer to question 3 on the time line below.

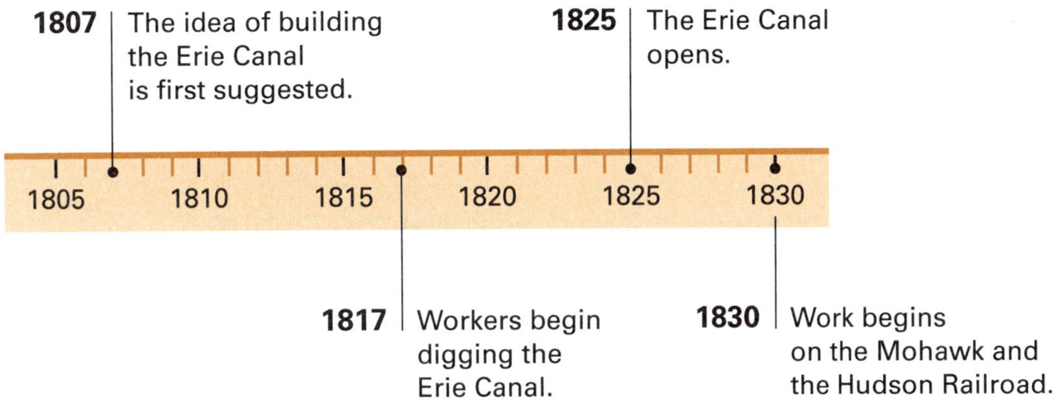

3 In what year did the Erie Canal open?

A 1807 **C** 1825
B 1817 **D** 1830

HINT Read the information given for each date on the time line. Pick the year that gives the information needed to answer the question.

---

4 A **patriot** is best defined as a person who

A moves to one country from another
B loves his or her country
C buys goods or services
D has always lived in the same country

HINT The people who fought for independence in the American Revolution were called *Patriots*. Think about why they were willing to fight.

5 When the Revolutionary War ended, the American colonies

A formed a new nation
B became part of Great Britain
C formed 13 separate nations
D became part of Canada

HINT Think about why the Revolutionary War was fought. What was the goal of the American Colonies?

Answers
3 Ⓐ Ⓑ Ⓒ Ⓓ
4 Ⓐ Ⓑ Ⓒ Ⓓ
5 Ⓐ Ⓑ Ⓒ Ⓓ

Go On

Directions: **Now you will answer a constructed-response question based on the history of the United States and New York. Write your answers in the space provided.**

Base your answers to questions 6 through 8 on the chart below.

Travel Between Albany and Buffalo in the 1840s

	Railroad	Erie Canal
Average Cost (per passenger)	$10.00	$6.50
Average Length of Time	15 hours	10 days

6 Which method of travel was faster? ______________________ [1]

HINT Look at the lengths of time on the chart for the railroad and the Erie Canal. There are 24 hours in 1 day. Which method of travel takes less time?

7 Which method of travel was less expensive? ______________________ [1]

HINT Cost of travel for each method is given in *dollars* and *cents*. Compare the dollar figures, *10* and *6*. Which is less?

8 Most travelers took the railroad. What conclusion can you draw from this fact?

____

____

______________________ [2]

HINT What made travel by railroad better? What made travel by canal boat better? Which was the better way to travel for most people?

Stop

STANDARD 2 World History

Directions: **In this section you will answer questions based on world history. Questions 1 through 5 are followed by four choices. Read each question carefully. Decide which choice is the correct answer. Mark your answer at the bottom of the page by filling in the circle that has the same letter as the answer you have chosen.**

1 Major Chinese inventions include silk fabric, paper, and moveable type for printing. What conclusion can you draw from this statement?

A Moveable type was invented in Africa.

B Paper was invented in Europe.

C A civilization did not develop in China.

D A civilization developed in China.

HINT Remember that a civilization is a culture that has reached a high stage of development.

2 Movement from one geographical region to another is called

A distant location

B exact location

C place

D migration

HINT Sometimes words that look alike have similar meanings. Think about words used to refer to people who move from one geographical region to another. Do any of these sound like the choices above?

Answers

1 Ⓐ Ⓑ Ⓒ Ⓓ

2 Ⓐ Ⓑ Ⓒ Ⓓ

Go On

3 The first Europeans who sailed to reach the Americas were searching for a faster way to

A Africa　　**C** Antarctica

B Asia　　**D** Australia

HINT Earlier Europeans had found ways to reach this place by traveling over land to the East. What continent lies to the east of Europe?

4 Which map shows the route that the Pilgrims on the *Mayflower* followed in 1620?

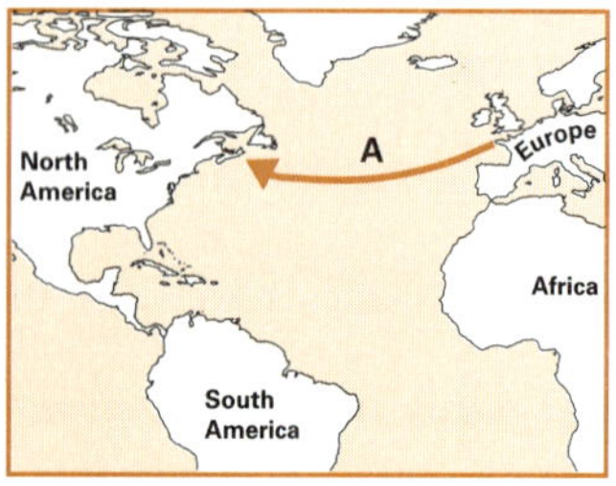

A

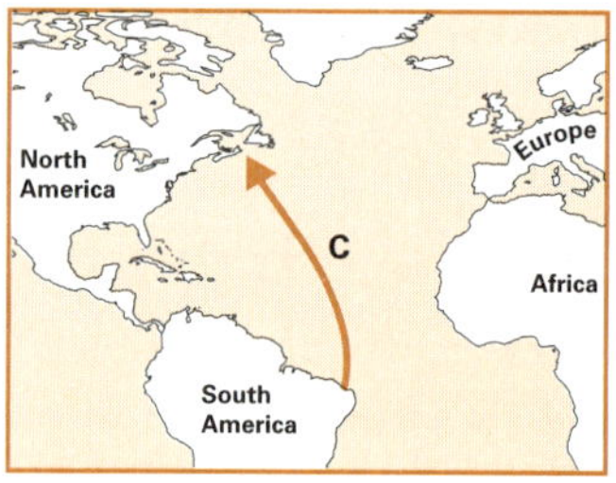

C

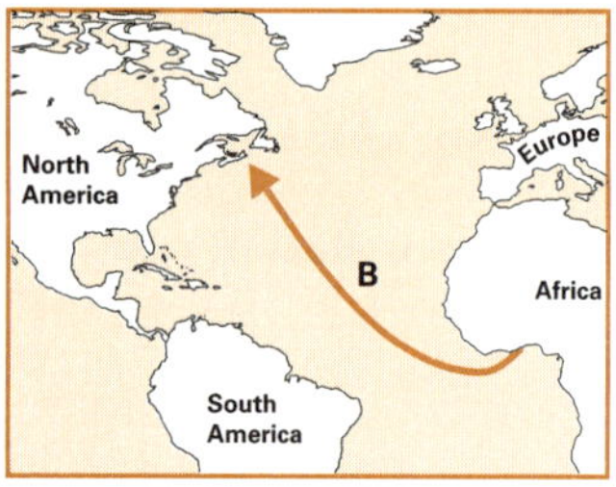

B

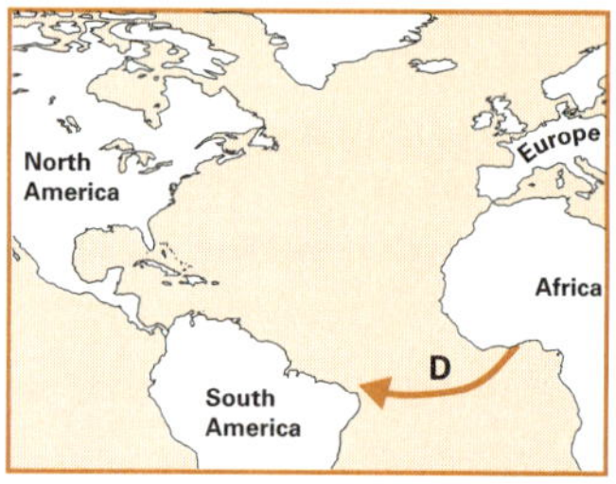

D

HINT The Pilgrims sailed to our continent from England. Where is England located? Trace the route that begins from that place.

---

5 Which best describes the way of life of the earliest inhabitants of North America?

A sailors　　**C** traders

B hunters　　**D** farmers

HINT Remember that the earliest inhabitants followed the movement of large animal herds.

Answers

3 Ⓐ Ⓑ Ⓒ Ⓓ　　5 Ⓐ Ⓑ Ⓒ Ⓓ

4 Ⓐ Ⓑ Ⓒ Ⓓ

Go On

Directions: **Now you will answer a constructed-response question based on world history. Write your answers in the space provided.**

Base your answers to questions 6 through 8 on the time line below.

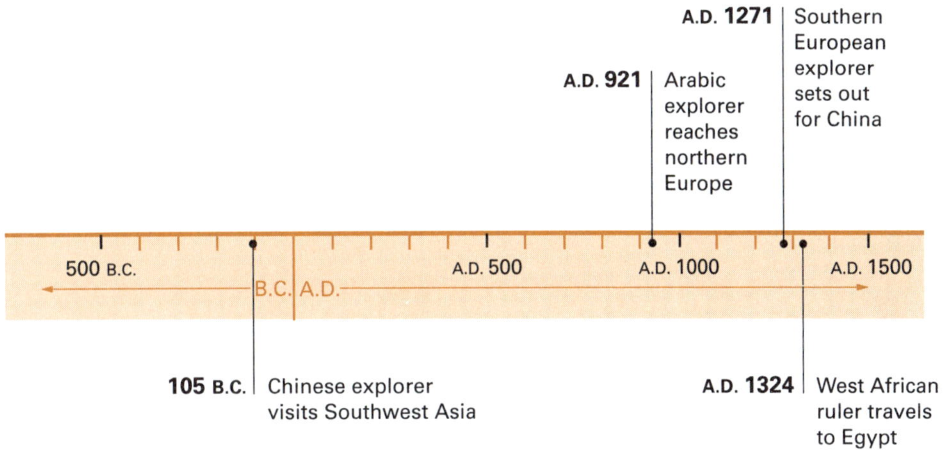

6 In what year did an Arabic explorer reach northern Europe? ____________ [1]

HINT Find the group of words on the time line that contains the information stated in the question.

7 What is the earliest historical event shown on the time line? ____________

____________ [1]

HINT Read a time line the same way you read a sentence (from left to right). The earliest date is like the first word in a sentence.

8 What is the latest historical event shown on the time line? ____________

____________ [1]

HINT The latest date on a time line is like the last word in a sentence.

Stop

STANDARD 3 Geography

Directions: **In this section you will answer questions based on geography. Questions 1 through 5 are followed by four choices. Read each question carefully. Decide which choice is the correct answer. Mark your answer at the bottom of the page by filling in the circle that has the same letter as the answer you have chosen.**

1 What is the name of the imaginary line that divides Earth into northern and southern hemispheres?

A the North Pole

B the Equator

C the Prime Meridian

D the South Pole

HINT The line divides Earth into parts that are about equal. Look for a choice that has part of the word *equal* in it.

2 Which of these is a **continent**?

A Albany

B California

C England

D Asia

HINT Consider what makes up a continent. Eliminate any choices that are not continents, such as: cities, states, or countries.

Answers

1 Ⓐ Ⓑ Ⓒ Ⓓ

2 Ⓐ Ⓑ Ⓒ Ⓓ

Go On

3 Which would be best suited to the development of an agricultural community?

A a desert
B a rain forest
C a plain
D a mountain

HINT Areas best suited to agriculture (farming) are on level land, receive enough rain, and get plenty of sunlight. Use these clues to eliminate choices.

Base your answers to questions 4 and 5 on the map of New York State below.

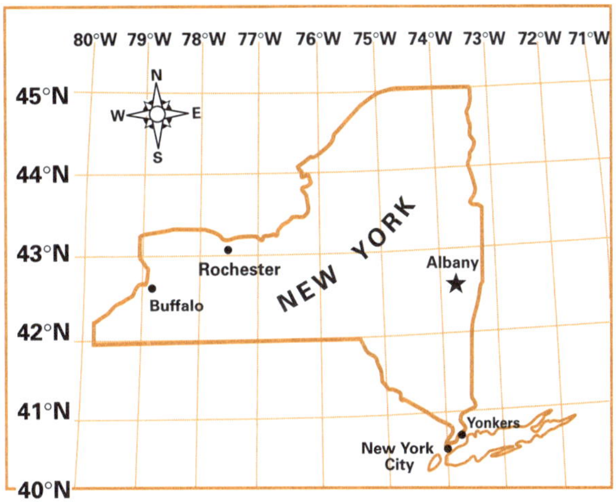

4 Between which two latitude lines does New York State lie?

A 35°N and 40°N
B 40°N and 45°N
C 42°N and 44°N
D 44°N and 45°N

HINT Find the line that is closest to New York's southern border. Find the line closest to its northern border.

5 Which city on the map is closest to 79°W longitude?

A Buffalo
B Yonkers
C Rochester
D Albany

HINT Find 79°W at the top and follow that line until you locate the answer.

Answers
3 Ⓐ Ⓑ Ⓒ Ⓓ
4 Ⓐ Ⓑ Ⓒ Ⓓ
5 Ⓐ Ⓑ Ⓒ Ⓓ

Go On

Directions: **Now you will answer a constructed-response question based on geography. Write your answers in the space provided.**

Base your answers to questions 6 through 8 on the bar graph below.

Percentage of Population Increase Between 1980 and 1990

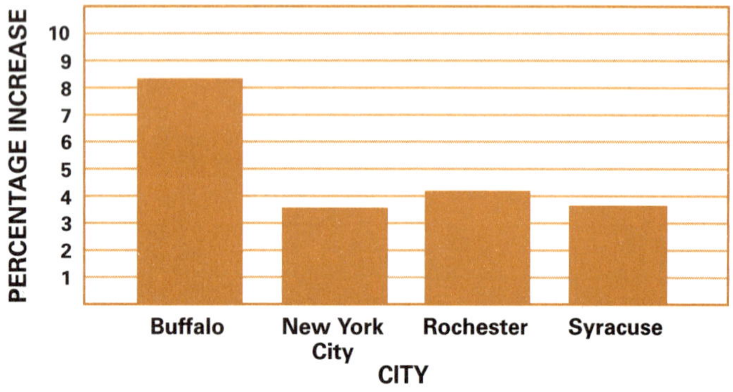

—from *The World Almanac of the U.S.A.* (adapted)

6 Which city shown on the bar graph had the greatest increase in population between 1980 and 1990? ______________________ [1]

HINT Compare the lengths of the bars on the graph. The longest bar represents the highest percentage (or number).

7 Which city shown on the bar graph had the smallest increase in population between 1980 and 1990? ______________________ [1]

HINT The shortest bar represents the smallest percentage (or number).

8 Write a statement comparing the population in these four cities in New York. Use the information given. ______________________

____

______________________ [2]

HINT Look at the percentages given for every city. Ask yourself: "Did population increase, decrease, or vary from city to city?"

Stop

STANDARD 4 Economics

Directions: **In this section you will answer questions based on economics. Questions 1 through 5 are followed by four choices. Read each question carefully. Decide which choice is the correct answer. Mark your answer at the bottom of the page by filling in the circle that has the same letter as the answer you have chosen.**

1 Which of these farm products is most important to New York State's economy?

A beef

B oranges

C wheat

D cheese

HINT Read the question carefully. The key word is "most." New York gets about three-fifths of its farm income from *dairy* products. Dairy products come from milk.

2 Goods and service that people must have are called

A wants

B scarcity

C needs

D industry

HINT Think about the meaning of the word *must*. Try fitting each choice into this sentence: "A human being ________ water to live."

Answers

1 Ⓐ Ⓑ Ⓒ Ⓓ
2 Ⓐ Ⓑ Ⓒ Ⓓ

Go On

Base your answer to question 3 on the pictures below.

3 Which statement is best illustrated by the objects pictured?

A The 1800s saw important changes in transportation.

B Immigrants came to the United States to find jobs.

C Immigrants came to the United States to escape injustice.

D The 1900s saw important changes in communications.

HINT First, eliminate the unrelated choices. Then, think about the purpose of the objects shown.

---

4 Which is a human resource used to meet needs and wants?

A rivers

B workers

C money

D oil

HINT The word *human* refers to people. Which resource listed is most closely related to the word "people"?

5 Which trend was an effect of the Industrial Revolution?

A People moved from farms to cities to find jobs.

B People moved from cities to farms to find jobs.

C People left cities and moved to farms.

D Most young Americans took jobs as farmers.

HINT Three of the four choices say the same thing in different ways. Look for the one choice that says the opposite of the other three.

Answers

3 Ⓐ Ⓑ Ⓒ Ⓓ   5 Ⓐ Ⓑ Ⓒ Ⓓ

4 Ⓐ Ⓑ Ⓒ Ⓓ

Go On

Directions: **Now you will answer a constructed-response question based on economics. Write your answers in the space provided.**

Base your answers to questions 6 through 8 on the pie chart below.

Percentage of Workforce Employed in New York Industries in 1994

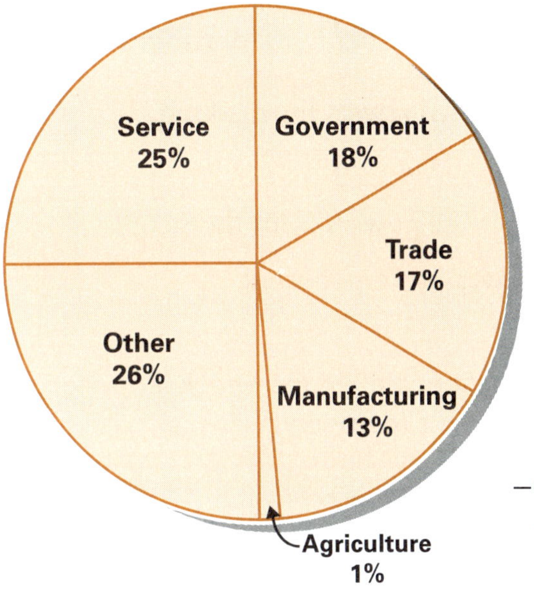

—from *The World Almanac of the U.S.A.* (adapted)

6 What percentage of New Yorkers held jobs in Government? ____________ [1]

HINT Find the word *Government* on the pie chart. Look at the percentage given under that word.

7 In which kinds of jobs were 13% of the people employed? ____________ [1]

HINT Find *13%* on the pie chart. Look at the kind of employment given above that percentage.

8 In which field of employment was the lowest percentage of New Yorkers working in 1994? ____________ [1]

HINT Find the section of the pie chart that is the smallest. This represents the area of employment with the fewest number of jobs.

Stop

STANDARD 5 Civics, Citizenship, and Government

Directions: In this section you will answer questions based on civics, citizenship, and government. Questions 1 through 5 are followed by four choices. Read each question carefully. Decide which choice is the correct answer. Mark your answer at the bottom of the page by filling in the circle that has the same letter as the answer you have chosen.

1 Which of these statements best defines a **democracy**?

A The government gets its powers from a king.

B The government has no powers.

C The government gets its powers from the people.

D The government gives powers to itself.

HINT *Demos* means "people" in the Greek language. Think about how this relates to the word "democracy."

2 What are the first 10 amendments to the U.S. Constitution called?

A the Articles of Confederation

B the Albany Plan of Union

C the Stamp Act

D the Bill of Rights

HINT The first 10 amendments protect basic liberties that the people have. Look for the word that is closest in meaning to "liberties."

Answers

1 Ⓐ Ⓑ Ⓒ Ⓓ
2 Ⓐ Ⓑ Ⓒ Ⓓ

Go On

3 The people of the United States vote for a president every

A 2 years **C** 6 years

B 4 years **D** 10 years

HINT Presidential elections were held in 1992, 1996, and 2000. What is the number of years between each of those dates?

4 The United Nations General Assembly meets in

A New York City **C** Tokyo

B Mexico City **D** Beijing

HINT United Nations Headquarters is located in a city in the United States.

Base your answer to question 5 on the picture below.

5 What symbol of freedom is shown to the right?

A the Washington Monument

B the Jefferson Memorial

C the Statue of Liberty

D the Bunker Hill Monument

HINT Look closely at the choices. The correct answer contains a word that is a synonym for freedom.

Answers

3 Ⓐ Ⓑ Ⓒ Ⓓ 5 Ⓐ Ⓑ Ⓒ Ⓓ

4 Ⓐ Ⓑ Ⓒ Ⓓ

Go On

Directions: **Now you will answer a constructed-response question based on civics, citizenship, and government. Write your answers in the space provided.**

Base your answers to questions 6 through 8 on the map of the United States below.

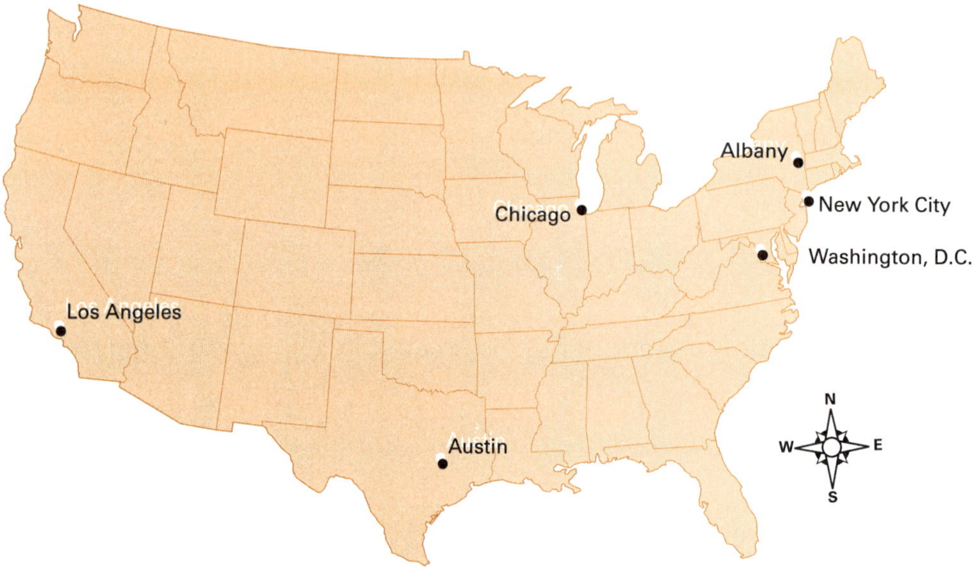

6 Which city is headquarters for the New York State government? ______________ [1]

HINT Many states placed their capital cities near the middle of the state. Find the city that is about halfway between New York's northern and southern borders.

7 Which city is headquarters for the federal (national) government of the United States? ______________ [1]

HINT The capital of the United States is located in the District of Columbia. Think of an abbreviation that might stand for District of Columbia.

8 In which city on the map would you find the government of the Borough of Manhattan? ______________ [1]

HINT Manhattan is one of five boroughs, or local units, that are part of the largest city in New York State.

Stop

Document-Based Question

Directions: The task below is based on documents 1 through 6. It will give you practice working with historical documents. In Part A, look at each document and answer the question or questions after it. Use your answers to the questions in Part A to help you write your essay in Part B.

Historical Background:

Forests once covered what is now the northeastern United States. Many Native American culture groups lived in these "Eastern Woodlands." The Iroquois of New York were perhaps the most important of these groups.

Task: For **Part A**, study EACH document carefully and answer the question or questions after it. These answers will help you write your essay.

For **Part B**, use the information from the documents, your answers from Part A, and your knowledge of social studies to write a well-organized essay. The focus of your essay will be the history and customs of the Iroquois culture.

Go On

Part A: Short-Answer Questions

Directions: The documents below show information about the Iroquois peoples and their culture. Study each document carefully. Then answer the question or questions that follow it in the space provided.

Document 1

At first, five major tribes, or bands of people, made up the culture group that we know as the Iroquois. The bands lived in different parts of New York State. Later a sixth band moved there. They were accepted into the Iroquois culture group. Each band had its own name. That name tells us something about the band.

Traditional Homelands

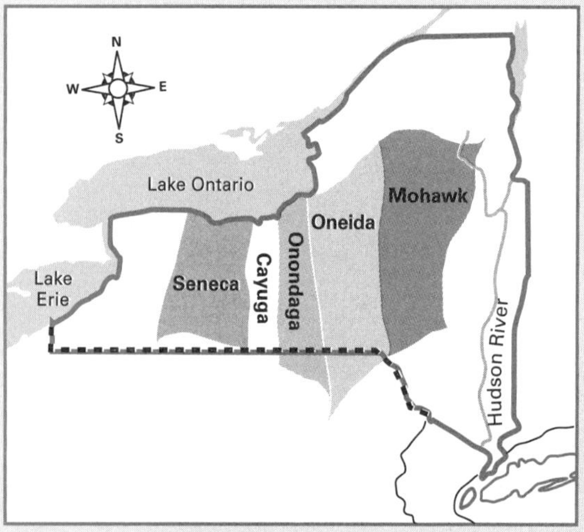

Mohawk	–the owners of the flint (a hard stone used to start fires)
Oneida	–the people of the standing stone
Onondaga	–the people on the hills
Cayuga	–the people at the mucky (soft, moist) land
Seneca	–the great hill people
Tuscarora	–the shirt wearing people

1 Which band moved to New York from another region and was accepted by those already there? [1] ______________________________

HINT The map shows the names of the five bands that had homelands in New York. What band's name does not appear on the map?

2 Which band probably lived on low-lying land near water? [1]

____

HINT Study the meaning of each band's name. Ask yourself: "What is the soil like at the edge of rivers, lakes, and streams?"

Go On

Document 2

At times, conflicts arose among the bands. About 400 years ago, a great leader appeared. He is known as Deganawida, the *Peace Maker.* The Peace Maker urged the five bands to live together in peace and unity. His teachings were written down in laws such as this:

"In all of your...acts, self-interest [selfishness] shall be cast away...Look and listen for the welfare [good] of the whole people, and have always in view not only the present, but also the coming generations [people not yet born]."

–from *The Thirteen Laws of the Peace Maker*

1 What values did the Peace Maker urge the five bands to practice? [2]

HINT Scan the introduction. The two values are stated in that paragraph.

2 What character flaw did the Peace Maker warn against in his laws? [1]

HINT A character flaw is a fault or a bad habit. Find the flaw mentioned in the Peace Maker's speech.

Go On

Document 3

Around the same time, another great leader came forward. His name was Hiawatha. Hiawatha traveled throughout the New York area. He persuaded leaders of the five bands to accept the Peace Maker's teachings. They formed the Iroquois League. As a symbol of the union, the Peace Maker planted a beautiful white pine tree.

> "Under the shade of this Tree of Great Peace...there shall you sit and watch the Fire of the League of Five Nations...Roots have spread out from the Tree of Great Peace...These are the Great White Roots, and their nature is Peace and Strength. If any [person] or any nation [band] shall obey the laws of the Great Peace...they may trace back the roots to the Tree...They shall be welcomed to take shelter beneath the [tree]."
>
> —from a speech by the Peace Maker

1 What values did the roots of the Tree of Great Peace represent to the Iroquois League? [2]

____

____

____

HINT

Roots support a tree and help it grow. What values would support the Iroquois League and help it grow? Find the answer in the speech.

Go On

Document 4

Strings of beads, called *wampum*, were very important to the Iroquois. Wampum was used as money (traded for goods). Giving wampum also could be a pledge. The giver promised to live up to an agreement. Often, these valuable beads were sewn onto a "wampum belt," like the one shown below.

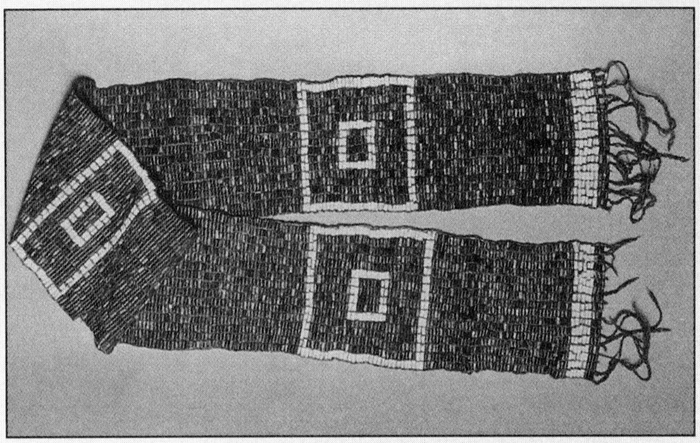

1 In what way was wampum like money? [1]

HINT Ask yourself: "What do I receive in return for money?"

2 What might be a reason why the Iroquois would sew a wampum belt like the one shown? [1]

HINT Look back at the paragraph. How do you think the Iroquois felt about wampum?

Go On

Document 5

A longhouse was the basic social unit of Iroquois culture. Clans [related families] lived together in one of these large log homes.

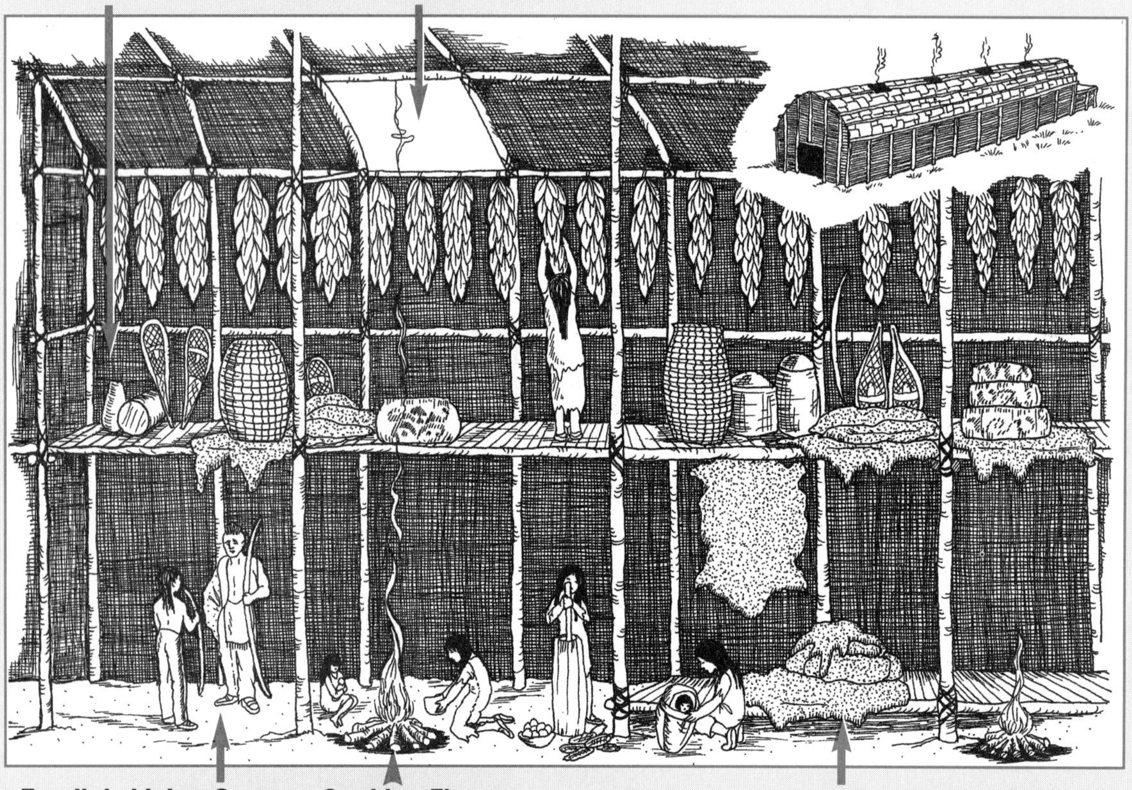

"...one of the rules to live in a community like that was to get along in harmony [peace]."
—Alice Papineau of the Onondaga tribe

1 How do you know that residents of a longhouse were honest? Use details from the picture and text to support your answer. [2]

____

____

____

HINT

Look at the areas where residents stored their goods. Finish this sentence: "Goods were stored in areas that _________ ."

Go On

Document 6

The Iroquois thought of their League as a symbolic longhouse. The bands lived in harmony "under its roof." A Grand Council, led by a *sachem* (leader), made decisions on matters that affected all "residents" who belonged to the League. Both men and women played important roles.

Gender Roles in Iroquois Culture

Women	Men
• chose a "clan mother" • each clan mother chose a male clan member to serve on Grand Council	• served on Grand Council • chose the sachem • discussed disputes in Council • together decided on peaceful solutions

1 Why was the role women played in the government of the Iroquois League important? [1]

HINT Ask yourself: "How did a man get appointed to the Grand Council?"

2 Why was the role that men played in the government of the Iroquois League important? [1]

HINT Ask yourself: "What effect did a decision resolving a dispute have on members of the Iroquois League?"

Go On

Part B: Essay

Directions: Write a well-developed essay about the importance of Iroquois culture. Include an introduction, supporting paragraphs, and a conclusion. Use the documents on the previous pages, your answers to the questions in Part A, and your knowledge of social studies to help you organize your ideas.

In your essay, remember to discuss:

- who the Iroquois were
- the Peace Maker's values and the Tree of Great Peace
- the Hiawatha Belt and wampum as a means of trade
- the longhouse as a daily example of Iroquois values
- the role men and women played in governing the Iroquois League

Go On

Planning Page

Use this page to plan your writing for the essay. Your planning on this page will NOT count toward your final score. Do NOT write your final essay here. Write your essay on the next page.

HINT

Think about the essay topic. What information from the documents you have read will help you address this topic? List the documents you will include in your essay and what you will say about each one. Pull together all of the information you will need. You might want to use a graphic organizer to help you connect your ideas.

Go On

Now that you have finished planning what you will write, use the space below and on the following page to write your essay.

HINT

Remember that a good essay responds to ALL parts of the question. It also supports statements you make with information and facts from the documents. Do not be afraid to write about what you think or what you have learned, but always connect it to the documents.

Go On

Once you have completed your essay, look at the Writing Checklist on the next page.

Go On

WRITING CHECKLIST

Now that you have completed the essay, look at the following list and check your writing. Go back and make any corrections to your essay that might be needed.

- ✔ Did you use your planning page to help you organize your essay so that it is easy to understand?
- ✔ Did you remember to answer ALL parts of the question in your essay?
- ✔ Did you use as many documents as you could in your essay and make sure that you mentioned them?
- ✔ Did you back up all of your ideas and statements with facts and information from the documents?
- ✔ Did you express yourself clearly?
- ✔ Did you stay on the topic and not add any unnecessary information?
- ✔ Did you write an introduction that explains what your essay is about?
- ✔ Did you write a conclusion that sums up what you wrote about in your essay?

TEST

Now you will take a practice test that looks just like the New York State Social Studies Test. This practice test will help you prepare for the real test. You will see the same three types of questions that you just practiced answering in the Modeled Instruction part of the book. Now, however, these questions will not have hints to help you answer them.

Here are a few tips for taking the test:

LISTEN carefully to the directions that your teacher will tell you before you take the test. Be sure to read ALL of the directions in each part of the test. Ask your teacher about anything you do not understand before the test begins.

READ each question carefully. As you answer the questions, you may look back at the information given with the question as often as you like.

PLAN your time. You may want to glance quickly through the questions in the part of the test that you are working on BEFORE you start to answer the questions. Always be aware of how much time you have to answer the questions in each part of the test. Check the clock often to make sure that you do not run out of time.

PART I of the test is made up of multiple-choice questions. You will answer these questions on a separate Answer Sheet that your teacher will explain to you.

PART II of the test is made up of constructed-response questions. You will answer these questions in the book, in the space after each question.

PART III of the test is a document-based question. You will answer Part A of the question in the book, in the spaces after the questions. You will answer Part B of the question in the book, in the space given for the essay.

To get the highest score on the document-based question, remember to:

- organize and express your ideas clearly
- answer all parts of the question completely and accurately
- support your ideas with the documents given

Now let's take the practice test!

Go On

PART I Multiple-Choice

Directions: Each question in Part I is followed by four choices. Read each question carefully. Decide which choice is the correct answer. Then mark your answer on the separate Answer Sheet by filling in the circle that has the same letter as the answer you have chosen.

Here is a sample question:

S-1 Which is the largest city in New York State?

A Buffalo

B Rochester

C Albany

D New York City

The correct answer is **New York City**, which is next to letter **D**. On the Answer Sheet, fill in the circle for letter **D**.

Answer all 35 questions in Part I of this test. Fill in only one circle for each question. Be sure to erase completely any answer you change. You may not know all the answers, but do the best you can.

1 Monsoons are strong winds that blow toward the East in summer and toward the West in winter. Why did merchant ships from Europe begin their voyages to Asia in the summer?

A Asia is north of Europe.

B European sailors do not like strong winds.

C The monsoons would help the ship move faster.

D Asia is a great distance from Europe.

2 For centuries, wool from Europe was traded for silk from China. What concept is best illustrated by this statement?

A Culture groups in Asia did not like wool clothing.

B Culture groups in Europe did not like silk fabrics.

C Culture groups exchange ideas and goods.

D Culture groups do not exchange ideas and goods.

Go On

Base your answers to questions 3 and 4 on the picture below.

3 What historic event is shown here?

A the signing of the Declaration of Independence
B the surrender of New Amsterdam to the British
C Jacques Cartier meeting with the Iroquois
D the Pilgrims landing at Plymouth Rock

4 What historic object appears in the background of the picture?

A Independence Hall
B the *Mayflower*
C the Liberty Bell
D the Statue of Liberty

5 The first people to reach North America crossed a land bridge from

A Europe
B Asia
C Africa
D Antarctica

Go On

6 How did the Algonquin meet their needs in winter?

A They brought water to desert crops.

B They migrated, or moved, to a warmer place.

C They used toboggans and showshoes when hunting.

D They built ice houses called igloos.

7 What was the main reason pioneers moved west in the early 1800s?

A to find gold

B to build factories

C to own land

D to escape the War of 1812

8 The Iroquois lived in large buildings called

A skyscrapers

B longhouses

C apartments

D pueblos

9 Which European explored the length of a New York State river now named for him?

A Henry Hudson

B Jacques Cartier

C Giovanni Verrazano

D Christopher Columbus

Go On

Base your answers to questions 10 through 12 on the bar graph below.

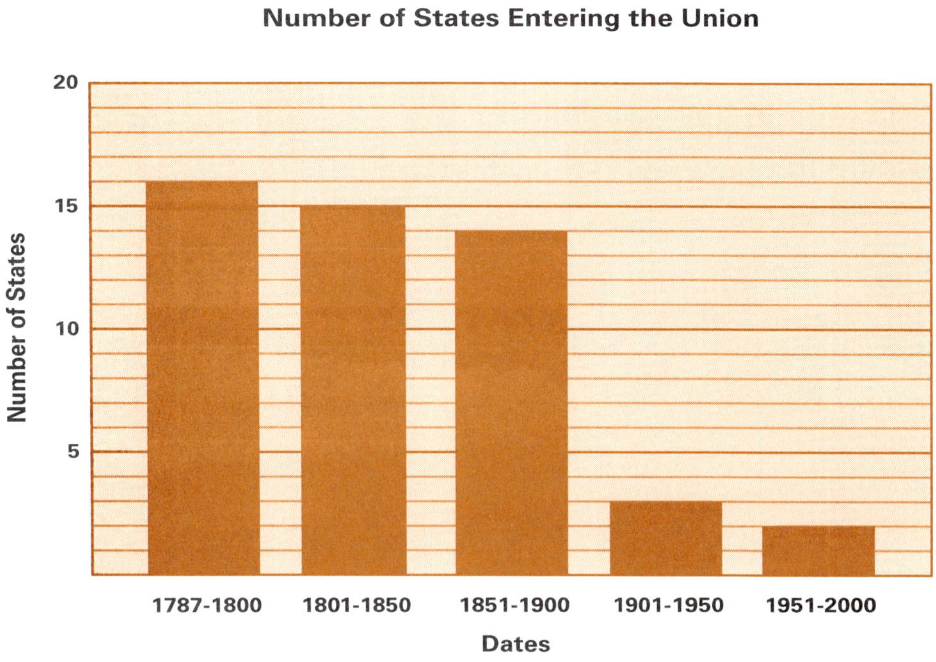

—from *The World Almanac of the U.S.A.* (adapted)

10 How many states entered the Union (the United States) between 1787 and 1800?

A 16 **C** 3

B 14 **D** 2

11 How many states were in the Union in the year 2000?

A 14 **C** 30

B 16 **D** 50

12 Which statement is true about the number of states that entered the Union between 1787 and 2000?

A The number kept getting smaller.

B The number kept getting bigger.

C The number got smaller and then bigger.

D The number remained the same.

Go On

13 A **colony** is a group of people who live in one land

- **A** and rule themselves
- **B** but move to a different land
- **C** and rule people who live in another land
- **D** but are ruled by a government in another land

14 On which map below does the shaded area best show the 1803 Louisiana Purchase?

A

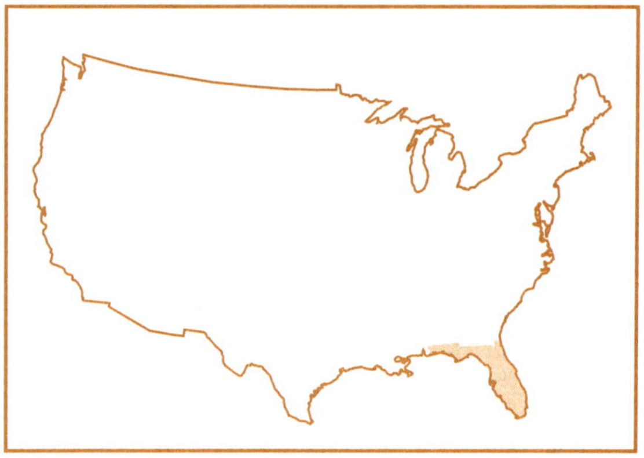

C

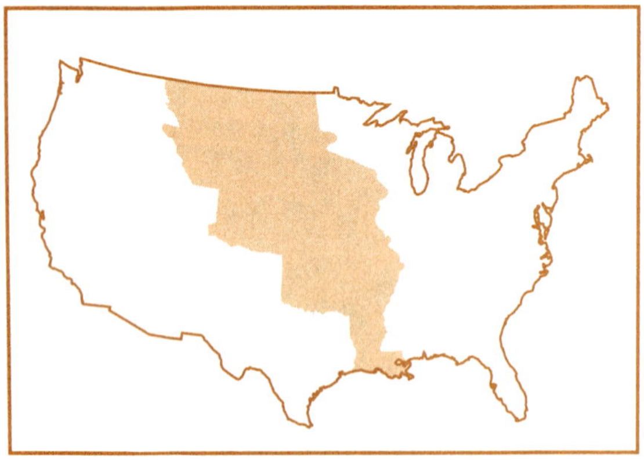

B

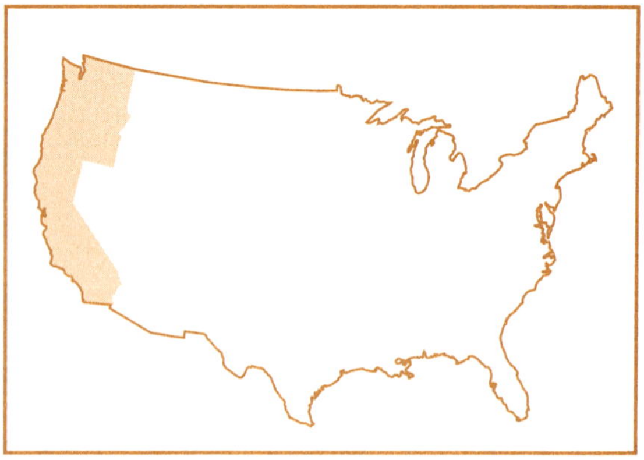

D

Go On

15 In the 1700s, most settlers in the British colonies were

A farmers

B sailors

C factory workers

D shopkeepers

16 What did Boston and New York colonists dump into the sea to protest a 1773 British tax?

A stamps

B molasses

C wheat

D tea

17 What does **revolution** mean?

A voting for new government leaders

B the complete overthrow of a government

C keeping the same government leaders

D doing away with all government

18 Who wrote the *Declaration of Independence*?

A Thomas Jefferson

B George Washington

C Thomas Paine

D Paul Revere

Go On

Base your answers to questions 19 and 20 on the map of Europe below.

19 Between which two cities can goods be shipped by truck, train, or plane?

A Dublin and London
B Dublin and Paris
C London and Berlin
D Paris and Berlin

20 How must goods be shipped from Ireland to the United Kingdom?

A by plane or truck
B by boat or train
C by boat or plane
D by truck or train

21 Which of these events happened in New York City on April 30, 1789?

A The treaty ending the Revolutionary War was signed.
B Paul Revere made his famous midnight ride.
C George Washington was sworn in as the first president.
D John Adams was sworn in as the first president.

Go On

33 A **culture** is made up of

A mountains, rivers, lakes, and valleys

B ideas, beliefs, and values

C lawmakers, judges, and presidents

D rain, snow, heat, and cold

Base your answers to questions 34 and 35 on the graphic below.

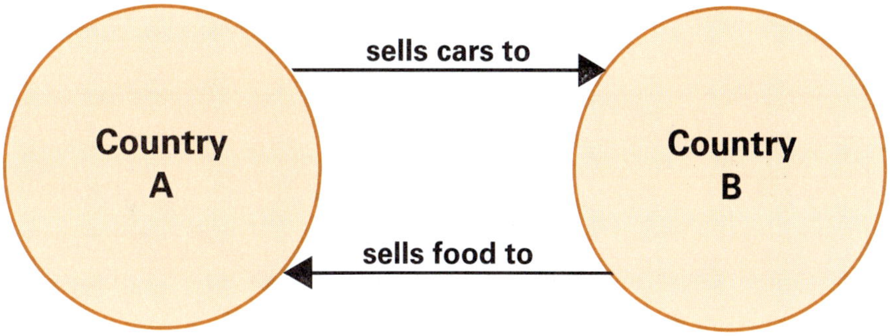

34 Which word best describes the chief economic activity of Country A?

A agriculture

B mining

C industry

D fishing

35 What concept is best illustrated in the graphic?

A conflict

B culture

C diversity

D interdependence

Stop

PART II Constructed-Response

Directions: **For each question write your answer in the space provided. If you want to change an answer, cross out or erase your original response. You may not know all the answers, but do the best you can.**

I. Base your answers to questions 1 through 3 on the line graph below.

New York Population

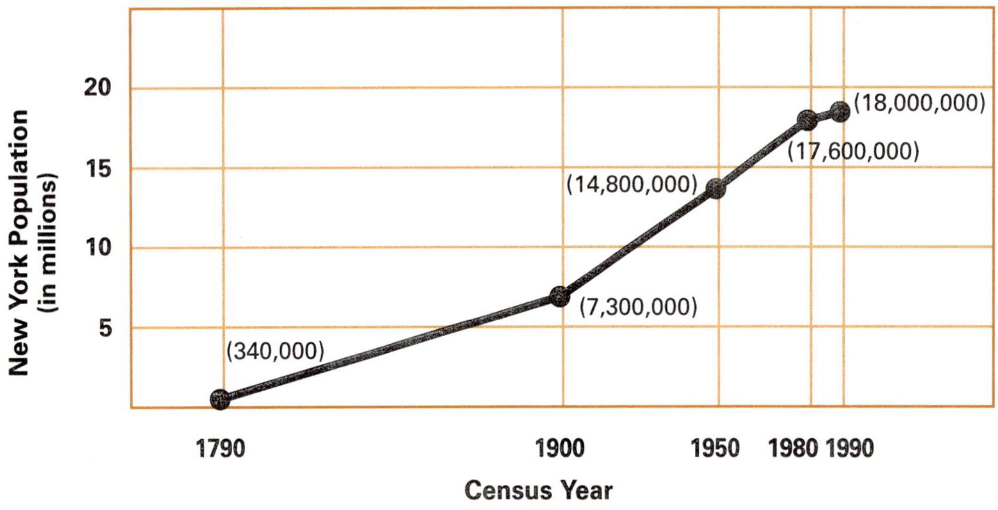

—from *The Time Almanac* (adapted)

1 What was the population of New York State in 1990? ______________________ [1]

2 Between which two dates shown on the graph did New York's population just about double in size? ______________________ [1]

3 Did the population grow faster between 1900 and 1950 or between 1950 and 1990?

______________________ [1]

Go On

II. Base your answers to questions 4 through 6 on the time line of the Revolutionary War below.

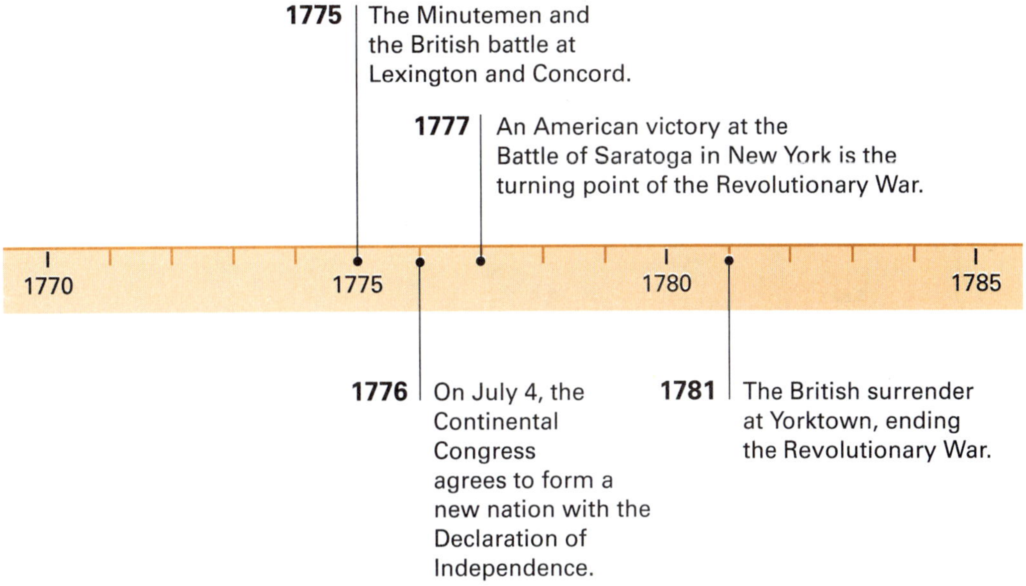

4 In what year were the Battles of Lexington and Concord fought? ______________ [1]

5 How many years passed between the signing of the Declaration of Independence and the end of the war? ______________ [1]

6 Which event on the timeline took place in New York State? Why was it important? ______________

____

____

____

______________ [1]

Go On

III. Base your answers to questions 7 through 9 on the map of New York State below.

7 What two cities are located at either end of the Erie Canal? ____________________

____ [2]

8 What two bodies of water did the Erie Canal connect? ____________________

____ [2]

9 In what direction did people from New York City travel to reach the Erie Canal?

____ [1]

Go On

IV. Base your answers to questions 10 through 12 on the reading passage and the map of northern Asia below.

The continents are the great land areas of the earth. The mainland is the principal, or main, land mass of a continent. A peninsula is a part of a continent that is almost completely surrounded by water. One side of a peninsula is connected to the mainland. Offshore islands also are considered part of a continent.

Northern Asia

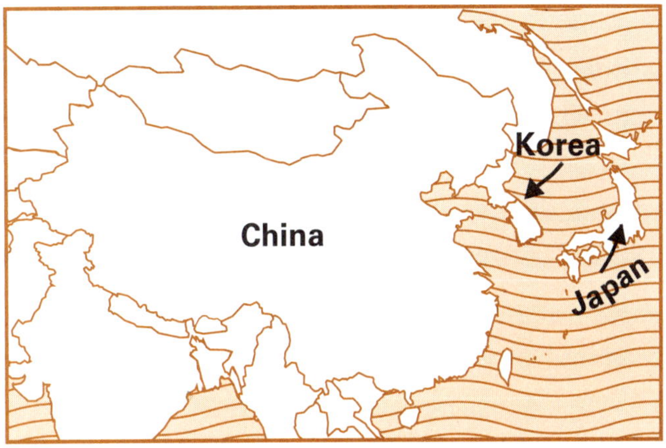

10 What is the largest country in northern Asia? ______________________ [1]

11 Which country named on the map is a peninsula? Why? ______________________

____

____

______________________ [2]

12 Is Japan considered part of Asia? Why or why not? ______________________

____

____

______________________ [2]

Stop

PART III Document-Based Question

Directions: **The task below is based on documents 1 through 6. It will test your ability to work with historical documents. In Part A, look at each document and answer the question or questions after it. Use your answers to the questions in Part A to help you write your essay in Part B.**

Historical Background:

> The United States has been called a "nation of immigrants." Millions of these newcomers first set foot on American soil in New York. Their story is one of struggle and triumph.

Task: For **Part A**, study EACH document carefully and answer the question or questions after it. These answers will help you write your essay.

For **Part B**, use the information from the documents, your answers from Part A, and your knowledge of social studies to write a well-organized essay. The focus of your essay will be the immigrants who entered the United States through New York State in the 1800s and early 1900s.

Go On

Part A: Short-Answer Questions

Directions: **The documents below show information about immigration to the United States in the 1800s and early 1900s. Study each document carefully. Then answer the question or questions that follow it in the space provided.**

Document 1

In the first part of the 1800s, large pieces of land in the northeastern United States were still unsettled. Offers of land for sale were made in New York State to emigrants [people leaving their country to move to another one].

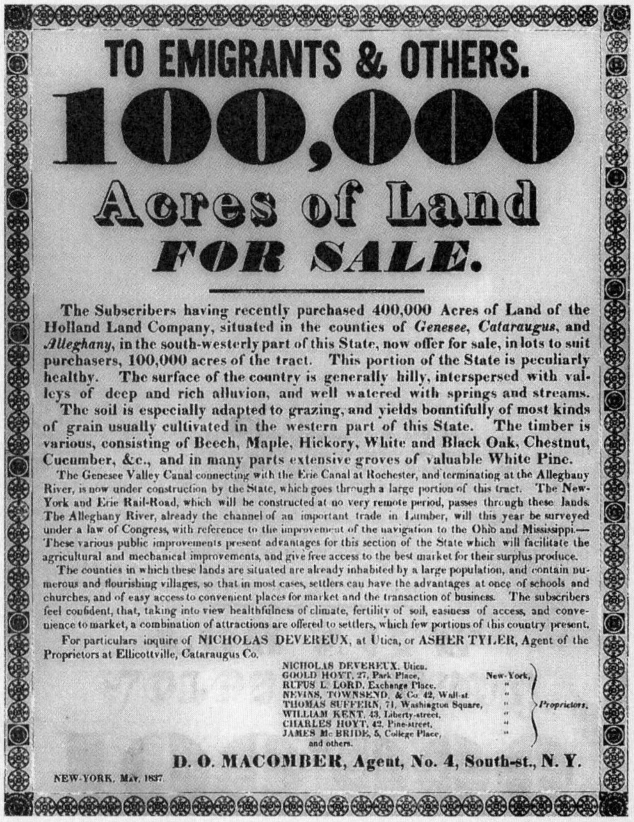

TO EMIGRANTS & OTHERS.

100,000

Acres of Land

FOR SALE.

The Subscribers having recently purchased 400,000 Acres of Land of the Holland Land Company, situated in the counties of *Genesee*, *Cataraugus*, and *Alleghany*, in the south-westerly part of this State, now offer for sale, in lots to suit purchasers, 100,000 acres of the tract. This portion of the State is peculiarly healthy. The surface of the country is generally hilly, interspersed with valleys of deep and rich alluvion, and well watered with springs and streams.

The soil is especially adapted to grazing, and yields bountifully of most kinds of grain usually cultivated in the western part of this State. The timber is various, consisting of Beech, Maple, Hickory, White and Black Oak, Chestnut, Cucumber, &c., and in many parts extensive groves of valuable White Pine.

The Genesee Valley Canal connecting with the Erie Canal at Rochester, and terminating at the Alleghany River, is now under construction by the State, which goes through a large portion of this tract. The New-York and Erie Rail-Road, which will be constructed at no very remote period, passes through these lands. The Alleghany River, already the channel of an important trade in Lumber, will this year be surveyed under a law of Congress, with reference to the improvement of the navigation to the Ohio and Mississippi.—These various public improvements present advantages for this section of the State which will facilitate the agricultural and mechanical improvements, and give free access to the best market for their surplus produce.

The counties in which these lands are situated are already inhabited by a large population, and contain numerous and flourishing villages, so that in most cases, settlers can have the advantages at once of schools and churches, and of easy access to convenient places for market and the transaction of business. The subscribers feel confident, that, taking into view healthfulness of climate, fertility of soil, easiness of access, and convenience to market, a combination of attractions are offered to settlers, which few portions of this country present.

For particulars inquire of NICHOLAS DEVEREUX, at Utica, or ASHER TYLER, Agent of the Proprietors at Ellicottville, Cataraugus Co.

NICHOLAS DEVEREUX, Utica.
GOOLD HOYT, 27, Park Place, New-York,
RUFUS L. LORD, Exchange Place, "
NEVINS, TOWNSEND, & Co. 42, Wall-st. "
THOMAS SUFFERN, 71, Washington Square, "
WILLIAM KENT, 43, Liberty-street, "
CHARLES HOYT, 42, Pine-street, "
JAMES Mc BRIDE, 5, College Place, "
and others.
} *Proprietors,*

D. O. MACOMBER, Agent, No. 4, South-st., N. Y.

NEW-YORK, MAY, 1837.

–from the *Collection of the New-York Historical Society*

1 What was one major reason immigrants came to this country in the 1800s? [1]

2 Look at the title of the advertisement above. How would people likely use the land offered for sale in this document? [1]

Go On

Document 2

In the 1800s, the Industrial Revolution changed economic life in the United States. More workers were needed for new industries that sprang up. There were not enough people living in the United States to fill all the jobs.

> "Industrious [hard-working] men need never lack employment in America. Laborers, carpenters, masons, bricklayers, stonecutters, tailors, and shoemakers, and the useful mechanics [people who work with or repair machines] generally are always sure of work and wages. Stonecutters now receive in this city (New York) \$2.00 a day,...carpenters, \$1.87$^{1/2}$; bricklayers, \$2.00; laborers, from \$1.00 to \$1.25..."
>
> —from *Hints to Emigrants from Europe*, a booklet written by the Shamrock Friendly Association of New York City in July 1816

1 What was another major reason immigrants came to this country in the 1800s? [1]

____

____

____

____

2 Where would immigrants seeking these opportunities probably settle? [1]

____

____

____

____

Go On

Document 3

Steerage was the section of a ship where passengers paying the lowest fares stayed. It usually was in the rear of the ship and farthest from the main decks. Passengers in steerage had the least comfortable, most crowded living quarters.

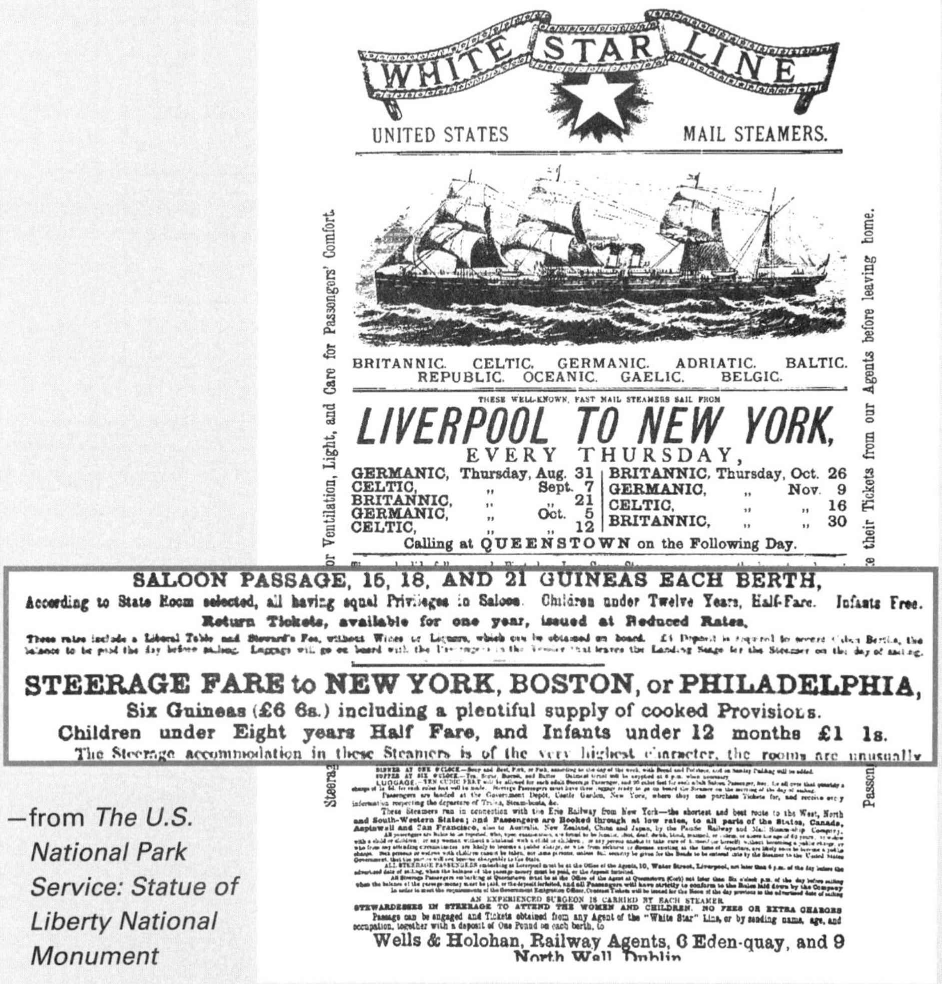

—from *The U.S. National Park Service: Statue of Liberty National Monument*

1 At what ports in the United States did ships carrying immigrants land? [3]

____

____

____

Go On

Document 4

The figures in the table below are for selected years between 1892 and 1924. The figures in dark type at the bottom show the **totals** for the 32 years between 1892 and 1924.

Immigration to the United States (1892-1924)

Year	Through the Port of New York	Total United States
1892	445,987	579,663
1900	341,712	448,572
1907	1,004,756	1,285,349
1914	878,052	1,218,480
1924	315,587	706,896
Total immigrants between 1892-1924	**14,277,144***	**20,003,041**

*71.4% of all immigrants who entered the U.S. between 1892 and 1924 came through the Port of New York.

—from the U.S. Department of Justice, Immigration and Naturalization Service, Washington, D.C. and *Annual Reports of the Commissioner General of Immigration, 1892-1924* (adapted)

1 How many immigrants entered the United States between 1892 and 1924? [1]

____

2 Why was the Port of New York so important to immigration during this period? [2]

____

____

____

Go On

Document 5

Hester Street is located on the Lower East Side of Manhattan in New York City. Many immigrants settled in the neighborhood around Hester Street when they arrived in the United States.

"For the first year or two they live huddled [crowded] together in the tenements [the least expensive rooms or apartments which often are falling apart]."

—from "The Bookworms of New York," *Independent,* January 23, 1913

1 What was life like for many new arrivals in the United States? Give details from the photograph to support your answer. [2]

Go On

Document 6

"In each of these [neighborhoods] there is a public library—so placed, not by design [plan], but by accident. Their readers once were mostly of one nationality. Now various peoples read in all of them. In the evening the men who work in the stores, the factories, on the docks, or streets, come to the library for the books. Those who have families carry home the volumes as paternally [protectively] as they lug food or clothing—perhaps more so if they happen to be very poor...most of them are spurred by a desire for leadership and they are picking education as a path to the goal."

—from "The Bookworms of New York," *Independent,* January 23, 1913

1 How did libraries improve immigrants' lives and futures? [1]

Go On

Part B: Essay

Directions: Write a well-developed essay about American immigrants' lives in the 1800s and early 1900s. Include an introduction, supporting paragraphs, and a conclusion. Use the documents on the previous pages, your answers to the questions in Part A, and your knowledge of social studies to help you organize your ideas.

In your essay, remember to discuss:

- why and how immigrants came to the United States
- what immigrants did after they arrived
- what the lives of many immigrants were like at first
- the efforts immigrants made to succeed
- New York's role in the history of immigration

Go On

Planning Page

Use this page to plan your writing for the essay. Your planning on this page will NOT count toward your final score. Do NOT write your final essay here. Write your essay on the next page.

Go On

Now that you have finished planning what you will write, use the space below and on the following page to write your essay.

Go On

Stop

STUDENT ANSWER SHEET

STUDENT'S NAME:			SCHOOL:
LAST:	FIRST:	MI	TEACHER:

Name grid (18 columns, each: ○ Ⓐ Ⓑ Ⓒ Ⓓ Ⓔ Ⓕ Ⓖ Ⓗ Ⓘ Ⓙ Ⓚ Ⓛ Ⓜ Ⓝ Ⓞ Ⓟ Ⓠ Ⓡ Ⓢ Ⓣ Ⓤ Ⓥ Ⓦ Ⓧ Ⓨ Ⓩ)

BIRTH DATE

MONTH	DAY		YEAR	
Jan ○	⓪	⓪	⓪	⓪
Feb ○	①	①	①	①
Mar ○	②	②	②	②
Apr ○	③	③	③	③
May ○		④	④	④
Jun ○		⑤	⑤	⑤
Jul ○		⑥	⑥	⑥
Aug ○		⑦	⑦	⑦
Sep ○		⑧	⑧	⑧
Oct ○		⑨	⑨	⑨
Nov ○				
Dec ○				

GRADE ③ ④ ⑤ ⑥

SOARING SCORES
NYS SOCIAL STUDIES
WITH DBQs
LEVEL E

TEST ANSWERS

Part I: Multiple-Choice

S1 Ⓐ Ⓑ Ⓒ Ⓓ
1 Ⓐ Ⓑ Ⓒ Ⓓ
2 Ⓐ Ⓑ Ⓒ Ⓓ
3 Ⓐ Ⓑ Ⓒ Ⓓ
4 Ⓐ Ⓑ Ⓒ Ⓓ
5 Ⓐ Ⓑ Ⓒ Ⓓ
6 Ⓐ Ⓑ Ⓒ Ⓓ
7 Ⓐ Ⓑ Ⓒ Ⓓ
8 Ⓐ Ⓑ Ⓒ Ⓓ
9 Ⓐ Ⓑ Ⓒ Ⓓ
10 Ⓐ Ⓑ Ⓒ Ⓓ
11 Ⓐ Ⓑ Ⓒ Ⓓ
12 Ⓐ Ⓑ Ⓒ Ⓓ
13 Ⓐ Ⓑ Ⓒ Ⓓ
14 Ⓐ Ⓑ Ⓒ Ⓓ
15 Ⓐ Ⓑ Ⓒ Ⓓ
16 Ⓐ Ⓑ Ⓒ Ⓓ
17 Ⓐ Ⓑ Ⓒ Ⓓ
18 Ⓐ Ⓑ Ⓒ Ⓓ
19 Ⓐ Ⓑ Ⓒ Ⓓ
20 Ⓐ Ⓑ Ⓒ Ⓓ
21 Ⓐ Ⓑ Ⓒ Ⓓ
22 Ⓐ Ⓑ Ⓒ Ⓓ
23 Ⓐ Ⓑ Ⓒ Ⓓ
24 Ⓐ Ⓑ Ⓒ Ⓓ
25 Ⓐ Ⓑ Ⓒ Ⓓ
26 Ⓐ Ⓑ Ⓒ Ⓓ
27 Ⓐ Ⓑ Ⓒ Ⓓ
28 Ⓐ Ⓑ Ⓒ Ⓓ
29 Ⓐ Ⓑ Ⓒ Ⓓ
30 Ⓐ Ⓑ Ⓒ Ⓓ
31 Ⓐ Ⓑ Ⓒ Ⓓ
32 Ⓐ Ⓑ Ⓒ Ⓓ
33 Ⓐ Ⓑ Ⓒ Ⓓ
34 Ⓐ Ⓑ Ⓒ Ⓓ
35 Ⓐ Ⓑ Ⓒ Ⓓ

Part II: Constructed-Response

Answer constructed-response questions in the book.

Part III: Document-Based Question

Answer the document-based question in the book.